T0032916

101 Things I Learned in Business School

Other books in the 101 Things I Learned® series

101 Things I Learned in Advertising School

101 Things I Learned in Architecture School (MIT Press)

101 Things I Learned in Culinary School, Second Edition

101 Things I Learned in Engineering School

101 Things I Learned in Fashion School

101 Things I Learned in Film School

101 Things I Learned in Law School

101 Things I Learned in Product Design School

101 Things I Learned in Urban Design School

101 Things I Learned® in Business School

Second Edition

Michael W. Preis with Matthew Frederick

CROWN
NEW YORK

Copyright © 2010, 2021 by Matthew Frederick

All rights reserved.
Published in the United States by Crown, an imprint of Random House,
a division of Penguin Random House LLC, New York.

CROWN and the Crown colophon are registered trademarks of Penguin Random House LLC.

101 Things I Learned is a registered trademark of Matthew Frederick.

Originally published in the United States in slightly different form by Grand Central Publishing Group,
a division of Hachette Book Group, New York, in 2010.

Library of Congress Cataloging-in-Publication Data
Names: Preis, Michael W., author. | Frederick, Matthew, author.
Title: 101 things I learned in business school / by Michael W. Preis, with Matthew Frederick.
Other titles: One hundred one things I learned in business school
Description: Second edition. | New York : Crown, [2021] | Includes index.
Identifiers: LCCN 2020047386 (print) | LCCN 2020047387 (ebook) | ISBN 9781524761929 (hardcover) |
    ISBN 9781524761936 (ebook)
Subjects: LCSH: Management. | Finance. | Commerce. | Business—Study and teaching.
Classification: LCC HD31 .P669 2021 (print) | LCC HD31 (ebook) | DDC 658—dc23
LC record available at https://lccn.loc.gov/2020047386
LC ebook record available at https://lccn.loc.gov/2020047387

Printed in China

crownpublishing.com

Illustrations by Matthew Frederick
Cover illustration by Matthew Frederick

9 8 7 6 5 4 3

First Crown Edition

Author's Note

An MBA is one of the most sought-after postgraduate degrees, viewed by many as a reliable avenue to a good job and lucrative career. However, while an MBA can help jump-start one's career and may speed professional advancement, it isn't the most essential factor for long-term success.

As often happens, when the majority of people figure out the rules of the game, the game changes. The paradigm of spending an entire career with a single employer or within a single industry is far less common than it once was. Those starting their careers now are likely to work for multiple employers and even in multiple industries over the course of their working lives. Thus, being able to learn quickly, adapt to change, and employ ethical behavior, passion, and savvy thinking in the face of new challenges is crucial.

Business school provides specific information, skills, and tools for tomorrow's businesspeople, but more importantly it instills a desire and proficiency for learning beyond the classroom. Further, there is no single discipline called *business;* it is, rather, a broad field of endeavor encompassing such diverse areas as accounting, communications, economics, finance, leadership, management, marketing, operations, psychology, sociology, and strategy. Those who confine their learning to one of these areas may limit their potential for advancement. Those most likely to be successful in business in the long run will be those with the broadest and most open understanding of it.

This book presents lessons in business that will be most useful to you, whether you are a student, experienced businessperson, beginning entrepreneur, or someone with a casual interest in the field. It may be many years before you have the opportunity to apply some of these lessons, but it is my hope that they will increase your understanding and help you navigate the interesting and challenging world of business.

Michael W. Preis

Acknowledgments

From Michael

Thanks to Sal Divita, Geoff Love, Kevin Waspi, Kevin Jackson, Joe Mahoney, Greg Kellar, Abbie Griffin, and Bill Brooks.

From Matt

Thanks to Tracy Arrington, Alissa Barron, David Blaisdell, Dick Canada, Paul Caulfield, Sorche Fairbank, Mary Helen Gillespie, Sung Jang, Jim Monagle, Roni Noland, and Sandy Parin.

101 Things I Learned in Business School

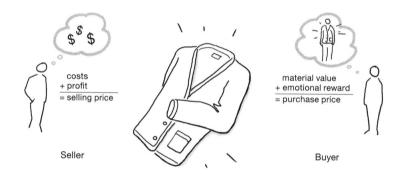

costs
+ profit
= selling price

material value
+ emotional reward
= purchase price

Seller

Buyer

Business is the exchange of values.

In a business transaction, each transactor assigns a higher value to what it receives than what it provides. A customer who buys a sweater for $50 values the sweater more than the $50, while the seller values the $50 more than the sweater.

The value of an item is thus not purely material or monetary, but may be emotional in nature. A value may also be anticipatory: one might "overpay" for an ice cream machine, for example, because of an expectation that it will generate future income. In this sense, business is sometimes defined as the exchange of current value for future value.

Business is a field of multiple endeavors.

Accounting: the language of business, which organizes and conveys information about transactions in monetary terms.

Finance: the management of money and monetary assets.

Marketing: the systematic identification of and response to customer needs and wants, including the coordination of branding, promotion, distribution, and delivery.

Production and operations: the coordination and overseeing of activities such as manufacturing and provision of services.

Organizational behavior: the study of how people act and interact in work settings; may include motivational strategies, corporate organization and culture, leadership models, group psychology, and conflict resolution.

Economics: a broad social science concerned with the production, distribution, and consumption of goods, services, and financial resources.

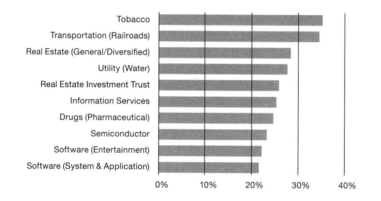

Industries with highest percentage of revenue kept after taxes, 2019
Source: Aswath Damodaran, Stern School of Business, New York University

Private businesses seek profit. Government-owned businesses seek universality.

Private, for-profit businesses are formed to earn money for their owners.

Not-for-profit organizations are created by private individuals and organizations to promote social causes, such as feeding the poor, operating museums, or teaching job skills. Monies gained through such activities must further the organization's cause, not be returned to its owners.

Government-owned businesses exist to serve universal interests. For example, it is of universal interest to have safe water; thus, a government entity might operate a water and sewer utility.

Some government businesses began as private sector businesses. Fire departments were once private businesses serving paying subscribers. But because a burning unsubscribed building threatened subscribed buildings, fire protection became recognized as a universal interest.

A common alternative to a government-run enterprise is a **regulated monopoly,** such as an electric, telephone, or gas utility. The government controls pricing and usually requires universal service—even to unprofitable areas.

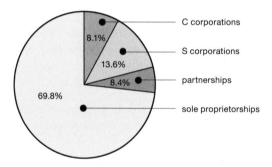

Business ownership in the U.S., 2014
Source: U.S. Census Bureau and Tax Foundation

Business ownership

Sole proprietorship: An unincorporated business owned by a single individual. The owner and the business are legally the same entity, although a separate business name may be used. It is the simplest form of ownership, and the owner is personally liable for all acts and debts of the company. Income is reported on Schedule C of the owner's personal tax return.

Partnership: The same as a sole proprietorship but with multiple owners. Partners' ownership interests need not be equal, but any partner may be liable for acts of the others. Liability is not proportional to ownership interest.

Limited liability company: A hybrid type of ownership that combines some of the simplicity and tax flexibility of sole proprietorships and partnerships with the personal liability advantages of corporations.

Corporation: A business entity that is legally distinct from its owners, who cannot be held personally liable for its acts or debts. The owners are stockholders. Stock may be privately held (e.g., a family business) or publicly traded on a stock exchange. **C corporations** pay taxes based on net profit, while **S corporations** pass some income and losses to the owners for inclusion on their personal tax returns.

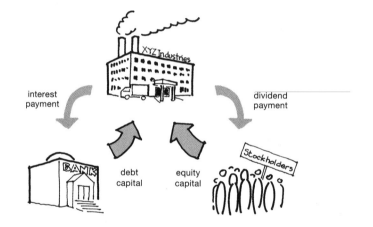

interest payment

dividend payment

debt capital

equity capital

Capital is money or "near-money."

Equity capital is obtained by selling a portion of the ownership of a business to investors—also called equity owners or equity partners. It is considered permanent capital because the funding provided by the investors never has to be paid back. Stock in publicly traded companies can be bought and sold on the open market. In small and closely held companies, there may be restrictions on the sale of stock by owners to other investors.

Debt capital is obtained by borrowing money. It is temporary in nature because it must be repaid to the lenders. Bonds and bank loans are two sources.

Stocks represent ownership. Bonds are IOUs.

A **stock share** is an increment of ownership of a corporation. Owners of **common stock** elect a board of directors to oversee the company's management, and are usually paid a dividend if the company is profitable. Owners of **preferred stock** typically do not have voting rights but are given preference over common stock-holders in the payment of dividends and liquidation. Some preferred stocks carry with them the right to be converted into common stock.

A **bond** does not represent ownership, but is used by corporations and governments to borrow money. With **secured bonds,** the issuer pledges specific assets as collateral in exchange for cash. A mortgage bond is an example. In the event of bankruptcy, a court-appointed trustee sells the assets and uses the proceeds to repay the bondholders. **Unsecured bonds,** or **debentures,** are not backed by collateral. In the event of bankruptcy, bondholders must compete with other creditors for repayment.

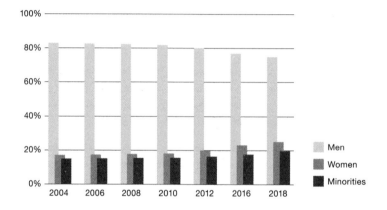

Composition of Fortune 500 boards
Source: "Missing Pieces Report: The 2018 Board Diversity Census of Women and Minorities on Fortune 500 Boards"

The board of directors

A corporation is required by law to have a board of directors, elected by and having a fiduciary responsibility to the owners (stockholders). A board should consist of experts in the industry and represent the long-term interests of the owners and other stakeholders.

A board governs at a strategic rather than day-to-day level. It establishes policy, sets direction, hires and supervises top management, is responsible for compliance with laws and regulations, and assures adequate resources for operations.

Directors of not-for-profit corporations do not represent stockholders, but the organization's membership as well as the general public. Some boards—non- as well as for-profit—consider themselves responsible to all parties interested in or affected by the organization's activities, including customers, employees, suppliers, neighbors, and even the natural environment. Such boards strive for a membership that reflects the diversity of the communities in which they work.

8

"In the future, there will be no female leaders. There will just be leaders."

—SHERYL SANDBERG, COO, Facebook

9

Philosophy of business and business philosophy

The **philosophy of business** is concerned with the nature and significance of business as a human endeavor, such as whether it is fundamentally an economic or social phenomenon, the moral obligations it has to society, the degree to which governments should regulate businesses, and the differences in business operations and meanings in capitalist and socialist economies.

Business philosophy refers to the values or approach of a particular company (e.g., "ABC Widget believes in educating customers before selling to them") or the dynamics of a market segment ("The widget industry demands balanced attention to product and service").

Mission statement

articulates the central purpose and
goal of an organization, to guide daily
decision-making and performance

Vision statement

describes what an organization ultimately seeks to become, or the ideal
society to which it wishes to contribute

An organizational statement that is impossible to disagree with might not be saying much of significance.

Organizational statements reflect an organization's philosophy. When drafting and evaluating a proposed statement, see if its opposite is obviously undesirable. If it is, the statement probably isn't saying anything particularly meaningful. For example, a junior college mission statement that says the institution "seeks to produce effective, productive citizens" is unlikely to have any real influence on employees or students, because no institution seeks to produce ineffective, unproductive citizens.

A meaningful statement asserts something specific, establishes priorities, precludes some possibilities, and describes what the organization does that some of its peers might not do: "We provide one- and two-year skills-intensive programs tailored to local employers' needs. Where possible, we provide core academic instruction for students transferring to four-year institutions."

Physical assets

tangible, measurable,
e.g., cash, real estate,
equipment, inventory

Symbolic assets

more intangible and abstract, e.g.,
social relationships, goodwill of
brand, influence in industry

People are capital.

Intellectual capital is proprietary information and in-house knowledge of technologies, materials, processes, and markets useful to an organization.

Human capital consists of talents, skills, and knowledge among employees.

Social capital and **cultural capital** refer to established human relationships, both internal and external to a company, that create and maintain value.

Brand equity is the additional value a brand name adds to an otherwise equivalent good or service, allowing a company to charge a higher price.

Institutional memory is unrecorded collective knowledge, techniques, tools, values, priorities, etc., developed in an organization over time. It outlasts the employee(s) who first developed it as long as there is significant overlap between outgoing and incoming employees.

Accounting and Finance

 Customer Service

 Human Resources

 Information Technology

Marketing

Operations

 Production

Purchasing

 Research and Development

Sales

A one-person business has departments.

Many businesses have similar concerns and responsibilities, and therefore similar departments. A department in a large business may have hundreds or thousands of employees; in a sole proprietorship it may be represented by a folder in the cloud and a few hours of work per month.

Honoring the universality of departments is essential to setting up a business and facilitating growth. Putting standards and practices in place that others will readily understand anticipates the eventual hiring of employees. Even naming and arranging computer folders and files by a universal, rather than idiosyncratic, standard can help growth occur more naturally.

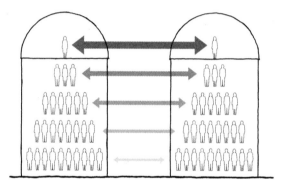

Department A   Department B

Functional silos can be dysfunctional.

The many disciplines in business are often organized and studied independently. This separation can provide intellectual and administrative clarity, but **functional silos** are not inherently distinct, as many business activities must be performed across them. The actions of departments and their employees invariably affect other departments, as well as the entire organization. The higher an employee advances within a silo in an organization, the greater the need to understand the activities of and interact with personnel in other silos.

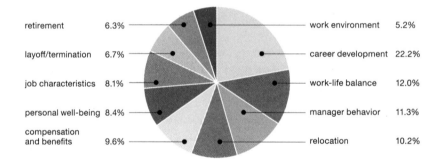

retirement	6.3%		work environment	5.2%
layoff/termination	6.7%		career development	22.2%
job characteristics	8.1%		work-life balance	12.0%
personal well-being	8.4%		manager behavior	11.3%
compensation and benefits	9.6%		relocation	10.2%

Why employees quit
Source: Work Institute, 2018

Staffing is more than hiring.

A high-performing organization doesn't merely recruit and hire employees. It actively orients them to the culture and goals of the organization, and turns them from outsiders into insiders. It gives them initial training to start their jobs and ongoing training to improve in them. It recognizes that giving employees opportunities to advance within the organization means they don't have to leave to get promoted, and the business does not have to restart the hiring process.

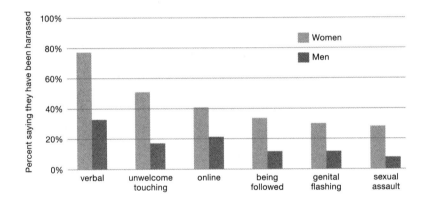

Workplace harassment
Source: Stop Street Harassment, 2018

The most difficult, time-consuming problems in business are not business problems.

Business endeavors are often complicated by human factors: misunderstandings, absenteeism, selfish agendas, ego clashes, personal business performed on company time, and more. Wise managers identify and minimize root factors in the work environment that contribute to people problems, and acknowledge and resolve the problems that do occur. They act as a model for others, knowing that their behaviors set a tone for the department or entire organization.

"If your thinking is sloppy, your business will be sloppy. If you are disorganized, your business will be disorganized. If you are greedy, your employees will be greedy, giving you less and less of themselves and always asking for more."

—MICHAEL GERBER, business consultant and author

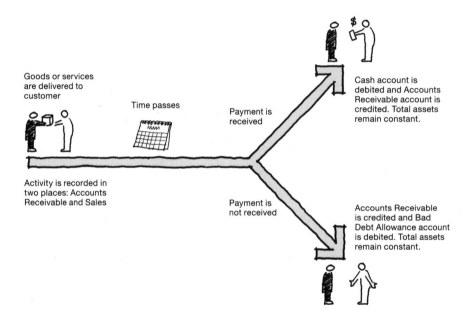

Goods or services are delivered to customer

Time passes

Payment is received

Cash account is debited and Accounts Receivable account is credited. Total assets remain constant.

Activity is recorded in two places: Accounts Receivable and Sales

Payment is not received

Accounts Receivable is credited and Bad Debt Allowance account is debited. Total assets remain constant.

Accrual accounting

Cash versus accrual accounting

Cash accounting shows income and expenses at the time monies are received or paid out. It works best in small organizations, such as sole proprietorships.

Accrual accounting is more complex, but it provides a clear snapshot of a company's financial status at any given time by accommodating the frequent lag between when a purchase is made and when money changes hands. Every transaction is recorded in two places in a general ledger; a debit or credit entry in one account is offset by a credit or debit entry in another account.

When a business using cash accounting receives a utility bill, it records the expense when the bill is actually paid. In accrual accounting, the bill is recorded as a debt in Accounts Payable as soon as it is received. When the bill is paid, the company records accounting entries in Accounts Payable and in Cash.

Accrual accounting requires that some entries, such as bad debts, be estimated until final data becomes available.

Why debits and credits are confusing

A credit subtracts from an account, while a debit adds to it. To non-accountants, these terms appear to mean the opposite of what it seems they should mean. When we make a bank deposit, for example, our bank statement shows our account has been credited; so a credit seems to indicate an increase, and a debit a "debt" or decrease.

Our confusion is due to our perspective as customers of the bank: a bank issues a statement from its perspective, not ours. A credit on your bank statement means the bank owes you money. In the bank's books, the credit is a subtraction.

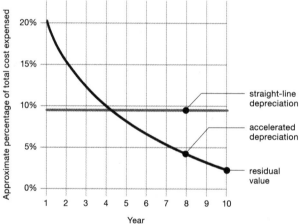

10-year depreciation

Depreciation makes accounting more complex, and more accurate.

19

The **matching principle** of accounting requires that any expense be matched to the period in which it helps a business earn revenue. Because a long-term asset helps a company earn money over many years, its expense must be apportioned over that period through **depreciation**.

Without depreciation, an organization's financial picture would be distorted: the entire cost of a piece of equipment with a life expectancy of 25 years would be expensed in the year it was purchased. This might make the company appear highly unprofitable that year and inordinately profitable in subsequent years.

Straight-line depreciation allocates an equal share of cost to each year, while accelerated depreciation expenses a higher proportion of cost in the early years, when an asset may be more useful and maintenance costs are lower. Short-term assets are expensed rather than depreciated, with their full value deducted from income in the year of purchase.

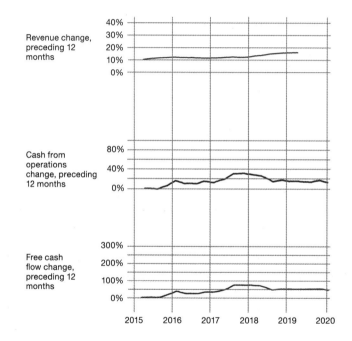

Walmart performance, 2015–2020
Source: www.fool.com

Use several accounting reports to gauge performance.

20

An accounting report for one period is useful, but static. A review of several consecutive reports can reveal trends and indicate if a business's condition is improving or deteriorating. Additionally, it helps to compare an organization with others in the same industry. Standard accounting reports include:

Income Statement (also called **Profit and Loss** or **Earnings Statement**): Shows performance over a period of time, such as a quarter or year. The last line of the statement shows net profit or loss—the "bottom line."

Statement of Cash Flows: Shows where money came from and where it went, for example, the purchase or sale of assets, and financing activities such as new borrowing and debt repayment.

Balance Sheet: Shows what a company owns (assets), what it owes to others (liabilities), and how much equity (amounts invested by owners plus profits and losses kept within the company) the owners have.

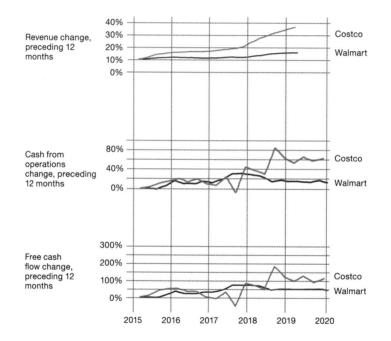

Revenue change,
preceding 12
months

40%
30%
20%
10%
0%

Costco

Walmart

Cash from
operations
change, preceding
12 months

80%

40%

0%

Costco

Walmart

Free cash
flow change,
preceding 12
months

300%

200%

100%

0%

Costco

Walmart

2015   2016   2017   2018   2019   2020

Performance comparison of Walmart and Costco
Source: www.fool.com

Financial ratios

Financial ratios reveal performance over time (**longitudinal analysis**) or in comparison to competitors (**cross-sectional analysis**).

Leverage ratios measure the financial risk in an organization by comparing debt to equity or debt to assets. A lower proportion of debt indicates less risk, although a stable business with predictable revenues can safely have a higher leverage ratio.

Liquidity ratios compare short-term assets to short-term liabilities. A high ratio indicates a strong ability to meet obligations, but a very high ratio may indicate that assets are inefficiently allocated; e.g., some of the money on hand might be better used for investment.

Operating ratios indicate efficiencies in day-to-day activities, e.g., the ratio of the cost of goods sold to sales, or net profit to gross profit.

Profitability ratios measure the ability to generate profits and include profit margin, return on assets, and return on net worth.

Solvency ratios measure the ability to meet long-term debt obligations by comparing short-term debt to total debt, and interest expense coverage.

Materials are "free"; it's everything else that costs money.

Business costs can be categorized very generally as **material costs** or **human costs**. However, material costs have human costs embedded in them. For example, the price of an item purchased at retail has embedded in it the costs of all previous labor, profit, licenses, transportation, tariffs, etc. When a product is traced back to its physical origin—as a raw material in the ground—material costs theoretically vanish.

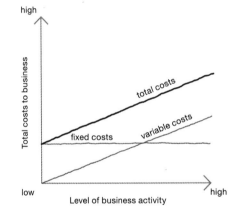

In the short term, some costs are fixed and some are variable. In the long run, all costs are variable.

23

A business's **fixed costs** are constant regardless of the level of business activity. For example, a hotel pays the same salary to a desk clerk whether one or ten guests register in an evening. Other fixed costs include depreciation, insurance, mortgage, and rent.

Variable costs depend on the level of business activity. For example, the cost of laundering linens depends on the number of occupied hotel rooms.

Fixed and variable costs both vary over longer periods of time. A permanent increase in the number of hotel guests might result in the hiring of additional desk clerks, making staffing a variable cost in the long term. If the construction of additional hotel rooms is undertaken, mortgage payments will increase to a new fixed level.

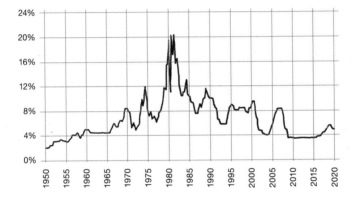

Average U.S. prime rate

An interest rate has three components.

24

The **real rate of interest** is the compensation a lender would theoretically require to make a risk-free loan in an inflation-free environment. It compensates the lender for postponing his or her own use of the money.

An **inflation premium** is added to the real rate of interest so that the principal (the original amount of the loan), once repaid, has the same purchasing power as when the loan was originated.

A **risk premium** is added to compensate the lender for the possibility that the principal will not be repaid. The risk premium is lowest for a lender's most credit-worthy customers, who therefore borrow at the lowest overall interest rate—the lender's **prime rate**.

A lender may also require a borrower to pay **points**—a fee at the time a loan is made—to cover administrative costs or procure a lower interest rate.

Annual Percentage Rate (APR)	1%	2%	3%	4%	5%	6%	7%	8%	9%
Approx. years to double investment	72	36	24	18	14.4	12	10.3	9	8

The Rule of 72

25

To estimate the number of years needed to double an investment when the interest rate is known, divide 72 by the rate. For example, an investment returning 9% interest per year will double in approximately eight (72 ÷ 9) years. The formula can also be used in reverse to calculate an interest rate when the time of return is known, or to calculate the halving of monetary value due to inflation: at 4% annual inflation, one dollar will have half the buying power in eighteen years (72 ÷ 4).

Greater accuracy may be achieved using 69 or 70, but 72 is more convenient as it has more divisors.

Monetary policy
U.S. Federal Reserve System

Fiscal policy
Executive and legislative branches

The U.S. government has two primary tools for influencing the level of business activity.

26

Monetary policy is the province of the Federal Reserve System, the central banking system of the United States. The "Fed" has the ability to influence short-term interest rates and the money supply. Policies that reduce rates and/or increase the money supply make it less expensive for businesses to borrow and expand, but can increase inflation; the inverse is also true.

Fiscal policy is the province of the executive and legislative branches. It refers to the rate, type, amount, and distribution of taxes and spending. It takes longer to adjust than monetary policy.

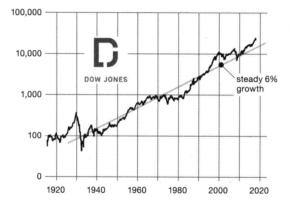

Dow Jones Industrial Average, inflation adjusted

The price of a stock is an economic and emotional projection.

The price of a share of stock derives from the economic value of the business that issued it. But determinations of value invariably contain subjective factors, ranging from personal biases to imperfect estimates of future revenues or debts—meaning that no economic value is established without an emotional component. Ultimately, the selling price of a share of stock is whatever a willing buyer will pay a willing seller, and is based on the expectation each has for the company's future.

While subjective factors may cause volatility in the value of individual stocks and even the stock market in the short term, overall stock market performance tends to be steady and predictable in the long run.

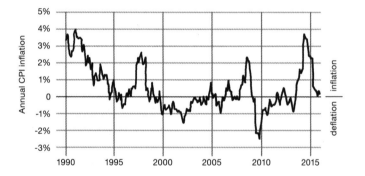

Japanese Consumer Price Index
Source: Statistics Bureau of Japan

Deflation can be bad for business.

Inflation is the gradual decrease in the value of money. It is a normal economic state characterized by slowly rising prices and salaries. Modest inflation can help spur business activity, as the threat of higher prices tomorrow may encourage the making of purchases and investments today.

28

Deflation increases the value of money, and therefore may seem positive. But it can be dangerous for businesses when it occurs widely, as it may lead businesses and customers to postpone ordinary investments and purchases in anticipation of better prices tomorrow. This can contribute to an economic slowdown, further depressing prices and stifling business activity. And as a business's income and profits consequently fall, it becomes more difficult to cover existing fixed costs, such as debt obligations.

When deflation occurs within a given industry or market segment due to a productivity increase, it is not necessarily problematic as all businesses in the category are affected similarly.

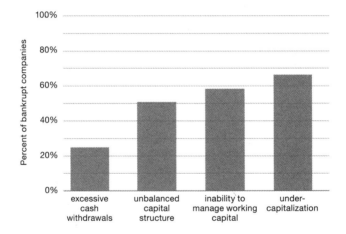

Financial management problems contributing to young firm bankruptcies
Source: Oilfieldpulse.com

A profitable company may be chronically short of cash.

29

A business typically makes a sale before receiving payment from the customer, while costs related to that sale, such as materials, labor, commissions, and overhead, are borne up front. Consequently, a business may be short of cash until payment is received. An especially fast-growing new company with rapidly increasing sales can be chronically short of cash, because the costs of growth (hiring and training new employees, acquiring new facilities and equipment, financing an ever-growing inventory, etc.) perpetually exceed the cash receipts from the previous, smaller sales volume.

Procuring and maintaining adequate capital is crucial, especially for a new business. Borrowing money costs money, but the alternative is worse: Undercapitalization is one of the most common causes of business failure. It can bring down an otherwise healthy organization.

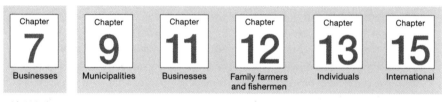

Chapter 7 — Businesses — Liquidation

Chapter 9 — Municipalities

Chapter 11 — Businesses

Chapter 12 — Family farmers and fishermen

Chapter 13 — Individuals

Chapter 15 — International

Reorganization

Bankruptcy doesn't always mean going out of business.

30

Chapter 7 bankruptcy is invoked when a business has inadequate assets, revenues, or markets to pay its debts and is unlikely to develop the ability to do so. It results in the company's dissolution. Assets are liquidated (sold) and the proceeds are used to pay overdue taxes, wages, and creditors. Any remaining cash is paid to stockholders.

Chapter 11 bankruptcy provides for the financial reorganization and continuation of a company that has insufficient cash to meet current debt obligations, but healthy assets, markets, or other indicators of profitability.

Most bankruptcies are voluntary; they are originated by the debtor. However, a creditor may file a bankruptcy petition against a debtor. A company forced into Chapter 7 by its creditors may file under Chapter 11 to prevent its liquidation.

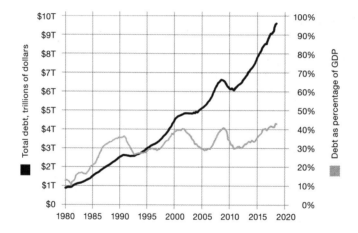

U.S. corporate debt
Source: St. Louis Federal Reserve

Why buy debt?

31

"Purchasing debt" is a bit of a misnomer: One who buys debt does not actually end up with more debt per se. Rather, he or she acquires the right to collect money owed by a borrower. Debts owed by private citizens and businesses to banks, finance agencies, utility companies, medical care providers, and other businesses can sometimes be purchased for pennies on the dollar. The lower the likelihood of collecting the debt, the lower its price.

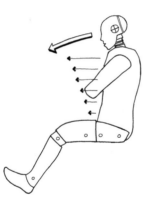

Those who think theory "isn't the real world" don't understand what theory is.

32

A theory explains real phenomena. It organizes diverse bits of information into generalizing patterns, identifies underlying reasons for why things happen as they do, and suggests the deeper nature of the things we know and those we do not quite know. Theories help transfer knowledge from one enterprise to another and suggest the likely outcomes of new and future situations.

Those who are averse to theory may thrive in business as long as the parameters familiar to them remain in place. Those who embrace theory are more likely to seek out, adapt to, and benefit from new situations.

33

"There's nothing so practical as a good theory."

—KURT LEWIN, psychologist (1890–1947)

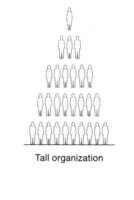

Tall organization

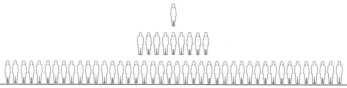

Flat organization

Span of control

Span of control is the number of employees reporting directly to an individual. The ideal span for a department or organization depends on the abilities of managers and workers, the nature of the work being done, and the similarity or divergence of tasks. Highly repetitive processes such as manufacturing can have a very large span, while creative businesses such as architecture and filmmaking may have a span of only a few persons.

For most businesses, a good starting range for determining span of control is around six to eight. When a sole proprietorship expands, for example, the owner will often find it necessary to create a new, formal layer of management upon hiring around 6 to 8 employees; another layer at 36 to 64; and so on.

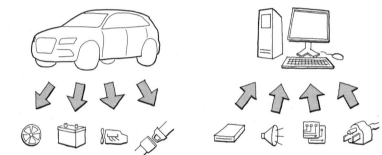

34

Top-down

Manufacturers dictate design
and production of components
to suppliers

Bottom-up

Inventors, manufacturers, and
suppliers create components that
others bundle into larger products

Top-down suits the known. Bottom-up suits the new.

Top-down management is authority-based. Information and processes originate in and are controlled by higher levels of management. It works best when a company's products or services are similar to those that were previously successful, when higher management possesses expertise or resources that lower levels do not, and when the cost of mistakes by inexperienced staff would be prohibitive. Top-down management can be predictable and efficient, but it also can become locked into outmoded practices.

In a **bottom-up system,** information and processes originate in the lower tiers, usually in an open-ended, ad hoc manner. It can work well in industries that are relatively new, in situations in which the lower tiers possess unique expertise or resources, and when the cost of errors is not prohibitive. A bottom-up system often generates alternatives that a top-down model cannot, but it can be chaotic and inefficient.

In top-down and bottom-up systems, flow can still occur in both directions. In a top-down system, for example, an astute, on-the-ground sales force may gain strategically useful knowledge of demand trends and competitor practices, or spy opportunities for product enhancements, new products, and pricing adjustments.

35

The higher one rises in an organization, the more one must be a generalist.

At the lower levels of an organization, employees usually have direct knowledge of specific activities. Production employees, for example, know how to handle materials, assemble products, test performance, and troubleshoot very specific problems. However, they may know little about other activities of the company.

Managers often lack such specific knowledge and skills but have generalized understandings of personnel, training, motivation techniques, evaluation, product distribution, compensation, and budgeting. A vice president will be engaged in still broader activities across more areas of the company, including long-range planning, product development, financing, and strategic direction. At the highest executive levels, officers and board members may be concerned with the philosophical direction of the company, the organization's mission, and the meanings of the company's brand in the market.

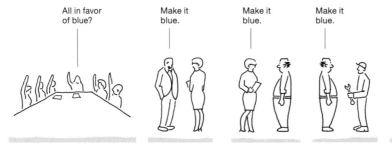

36

The higher one rises in an organization, the longer it takes to implement a decision.

37

Front-line managers can effect immediate changes by directly instructing workers: a sales manager can spontaneously redirect the activities of salespeople, and an accounting manager can institute immediate changes in bookkeeping practices.

But at higher levels of an organization, where employees are more concerned with strategic matters, decisions take more time to implement. If the vice president of marketing wishes to change the style of a product, considerable time will be required to perform feasibility studies, explore design alternatives, investigate technical considerations, and alter manufacturing methods.

Command, consensus, or consultation?

Command decision-making is the traditional top-down, hierarchical model. It is most effective when processes or products are similar to previous examples and when management has knowledge and experience that lower-level staff do not. It is efficient but can be over-reliant on old ways when a new approach is needed. Also, in a large, highly layered organization, command decisions by upper management may seem irrelevant to lower-level employees.

Consensus or democratic decisions are made by a majority of those most directly affected by the decision. They are valued for allowing voices into the decision-making process that might otherwise go unheard. However, front-line workers may lack the strategic vision of top management and be unable to base their decisions on changing market conditions.

Consultative decision-making hybridizes the preceding models. It is an authority-based model in which managers solicit input from the affected before making decisions. It is valued for allowing diverse voices while yielding clear, final decisions for which one party is accountable.

A manager may use all three styles, switching from one to another depending on the situation.

38

Finance

IT

Marketing

Operations

R & D

Sales

Subject-specific
traditional "smarts," usually within a universally recognized field

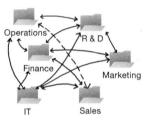

Contextual
skill in working among disciplines, or bridging between experts and the lay world

Political/social
reading human situations, solving people problems that affect "pure" business problems

Three types of expertise

An expert isn't always the person who knows the most.

39

Experts know a lot, but often it is better to know how to organize, structure, and contextualize knowledge than to simply have knowledge. Innovative thinkers don't merely retain and retrieve lots of information; often they identify and create new patterns and connections that reorient or reframe what others know.

Left brain
rational, analytical
linear
directly focused
detached observation

Right brain
intuitive
holistic
indirectly aware
immersive experience

We know more than we know we know.

You are riding a bicycle and it begins to fall to the left . . . which way should you turn the handlebars to stay balanced?

In surveys, most people answer, "to the right," but the correct answer is "to the left." And in fact, when riding a bicycle, nearly everyone will correctly and intuitively turn the handlebars to the left.

This discrepancy exists because our unconscious, intuitive mind is aware of things our conscious mind is not. Frequently, one has to be in action in order to know the right thing to do. Effective businesspeople often must make decisions on the fly, and must learn when to trust—or mistrust—their rational and intuitive judgments.

If all options appear equal, get more information.

When feeling stuck while weighing an important decision, it is almost always helpful to seek out new, objective information on any aspect of the matter—even if the effort or information to be gained initially seems of little value. Even the most modest new data on a market, client, or technology, when probed seriously, can provoke expansive new insights that point toward a more informed decision.

Be careful, however, that you aren't looking for excuses to put off a difficult decision. Sometimes there is a genuine need for additional data, but often one has to decide with incomplete information.

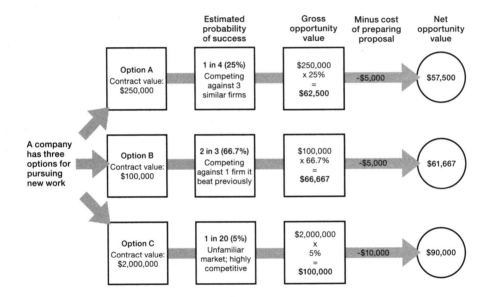

| | | Estimated probability of success | Gross opportunity value | Minus cost of preparing proposal | Net opportunity value |

A company has three options for pursuing new work

Option A
Contract value: $250,000

1 in 4 (25%)
Competing against 3 similar firms

$250,000
x 25%
=
$62,500

-$5,000

$57,500

Option B
Contract value: $100,000

2 in 3 (66.7%)
Competing against 1 firm it beat previously

$100,000
x 66.7%
=
$66,667

-$5,000

$61,667

Option C
Contract value: $2,000,000

1 in 20 (5%)
Unfamiliar market; highly competitive

$2,000,000
x
5%
=
$100,000

-$10,000

$90,000

Quantify the variables.

A **decision tree** compares the likely outcomes of various courses of action. It helps temper subjective considerations and guesswork, and guards against making decisions that are hunch-based or emotional. For example, a business-person who once failed in pursuing a particular market or client might fear pursuing that market or client again; a decision tree may help show if such fears are reasonable.

A decision tree cannot be entirely objective unless the variables and probabilities are entirely mechanical or rational. It may also be of limited use when the options have wide differences in probability or value. For example, a 100% probability of receiving $1,000 may be for many people a superior option to a 1% probability of a $100,000 payoff, even though the outcomes are mathematically equal.

42

Satisficers

- make good-enough decisions
- don't obsess over options
- move on after deciding
- more satisfied with outcomes

Maximizers

- try to make perfect decisions
- exhaustively consider options
- second-guess themselves
- more likely to regret decisions

A decision is the beginning of a process, not the end of one.

Circumstances rarely permit one to collect perfect data to support a pending decision. Even if perfect information exists, its potential benefits may be out-weighed by the time, effort, and expense required to marshal it. A good manager knows:

- when to make a workable decision versus when to attempt a perfect decision
- when to live with and when to correct a previous bad decision
- that a decision often becomes the right one in its implementation, and a right decision may become the wrong one if not properly followed up
- that a manager is properly judged on a long-term record, and that even the best decision makers make mistakes
- that a too-late or no decision is almost always worse than a bad decision

"Not to decide is to decide."

—HARVEY COX, theologian

44

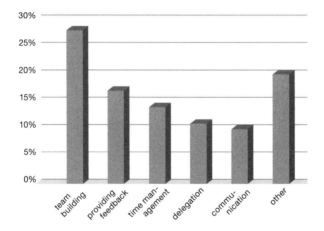

What skill does your manager most lack?
Source: People Management Report 2019, by predictiveindex.com

A manager's achievements are measured through the achievements of others.

Employees who excel in one aspect of a business are often promoted to supervisory positions. This is often a mistake, as the skills required to be a manager may be unrelated to his or her abilities or interests. A top lab researcher promoted to lab supervisor, for example, has to coach, mentor, manage, and help other researchers make discoveries. If the manager is poor at these new duties, the problem will be compounded: not only will the department be poorly managed, it will no longer have its best researcher making discoveries on the bench.

Management is its own area of expertise, distinct in many ways from the activities being managed. In very large organizations, top-level managers and administrators often lack expertise in the work being done, but are able to create circumstances that allow those under them to thrive.

45

Two views on good management

Good managers delegate. They think and work top-down. Their allegiance is to the big picture, and they leave it to those under them to carry out the manager's vision, determine logistics, solve day-to-day problems, and sweat the details.

Good managers work for those under them. They may think big, but they work bottom-up. They view their essential duty as actively facilitating staff. They identify and react to in-the-trenches needs and problems as, or even before, they arise.

46

Tell others the result you need, not necessarily how to achieve it.

Micromanagement can mean overmanaging the little things, but it also can mean overmanaging the middle things. Many good managers focus on two extremes of scale:

- **Identifying and communicating the broadest guiding values.** For example, achieve community consensus, honor functionality over aesthetics, and make sure the product is fun to use.
- **Identifying and communicating the most specific outcomes.** For example, the product can't be orange; it must be rechargeable in a half-hour, weigh less than 13 ounces, and have the power switch on the front; and all design work must be complete in nine months.

From there, the manager leaves it to staff members to engage the middle ground as they see fit. Telling others exactly how to do their work hampers their productivity, limits their learning, and takes away their initiative. Giving workers freedom to shape their work as they wish encourages them to be creative and become personally invested in the endeavor.

47

Magnitude
size of reward

Valence
importance of reward

Expectancy
likelihood of attainment

Components of extrinsic motivation

Most employees want to do good work.

Extrinsic motivation derives from anticipation of external reaction, including praise, recognition, money (positive motivators), or punishment (negative motivator). Positive motivators can lead workers to expect additional rewards for merely doing their jobs, while negative motivators may help get a task done but may have a detrimental effect over time.

Intrinsic motivation comes from a worker's internal sense of purpose, enjoyment of the work, and satisfaction of a job done well. Intrinsic motivation can be furthered by designing jobs to best suit employees, aggregating tasks in appealing ways, enlarging responsibilities, and allowing employees more control over their duties.

48

"At some point, you have to let go and trust your people. You sow the seed of trust by giving trust. I truly believe delegation begins with trusting others—followed by letting go."

49

—DAVID L. STEWARD, chairman and founder, World Wide Technology

Marketing
Any activity that connects or seeks to connect a business to customers

Branding
Crafting of the "felt" impression of a business among customers and the public

Promotion
A short-term, focused effort to bring attention to a business or product

Advertising
A commercial message to potential and current customers via popular media

Publicity
Public notification of a business or its activities via "objective" reporting

Do your marketing while you're busy.

It can be years from the time a new lead is cultivated until it develops into business. If you wait for business to slow down before initiating a marketing effort, it may be too late for it to help you get through the downturn.

50

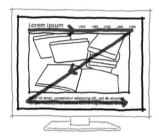

Z-pattern for most webpages

Viewers read the top, then scan diagonally toward the bottom to gain the gist

F-pattern for text-heavy webpages

Viewers read the top, then scan vertically on left side to identify additional items of interest

Don't leave the design of your website to the IT department.

A successful brand presents itself in every medium in a visually appealing, user-friendly way. A website is crucial to this. And because it requires a high level of technical execution—writing HTML code, coordinating links, manipulating video and still images, and constantly updating content—it may seem appropriate to give full responsibility for it to technical experts. But the essence of a good website transcends mere technical execution and includes a broad set of concerns, including projection of the company's brand identity, the psychology of user interface, and consistency with other media in which the company is visible.

51

Focus on the need, not the solution.

Customers don't buy a copy machine because they need a copy machine, or a coffee maker because they need a coffee maker. They buy them because they need copies or coffee.

Customers make purchases to solve problems. A good salesperson first seeks to understand the nature and extent of a customer's problem before offering a solution. Often, the right solution is very different from what the customer assumed. A good salesperson will even talk a customer out of making a wrong purchase, because in the long run the customer will respect the salesperson's honesty and may become a repeat customer. Further, losing potential sales in this manner may help you understand the direction in which your line of goods or services needs to evolve.

52

Feature   Benefit

A feature is a fact. A benefit is how it helps the customer.

Pointing out the features of a product to customers does not mean they will understand why the features are useful; one has to explain their direct benefits. For example, call forwarding and call waiting are features; never missing another call is their benefit. Benefits, not features, ultimately sell products.

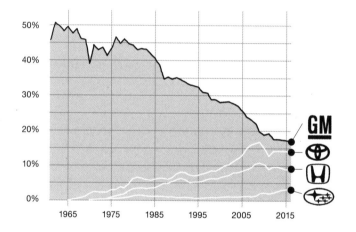

U.S. automobile market share
Source: knoema.com

Targeting the safe middle market is not necessarily a safe strategy.

When a market for a new product category is growing rapidly, selling average-quality products at moderate prices can be a viable strategy. As a market matures, however, customers tend to seek out either basic, low-priced products or higher-priced products that emphasize styling, quality, features, benefits, and exclusivity. Brands that continue to target the middle of the market with mid-priced products, without giving customers specific and compelling reasons to buy them, usually lose market share.

54

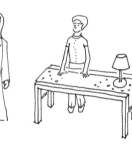

Customers do not make purchases the same way or for the same reason.

Marketing experts typically distinguish among consumers by age, geography, interests, income, and similar factors. They may use a different marketing mix of the **Four P's** to determine how to reach each segment:

Product: an offering's features, style, variety (e.g., cane sugar, granulated sugar, light brown sugar, etc.), packaging (single-serving packets, five-pound packages, etc.), and brand name.

Price: the list price, discounts, allowances, and payment terms.

Promotion: advertising, personal selling, sales promotions, and public relations. A product aimed at young buyers, for example, might emphasize Web-based promotion over print advertising.

Place: the venue for purchase and the logistics of moving products from manufacturer to consumer; for example, whether the product will be sold through authorized retailers only, in vending machines, etc.

Some experts use **Five P's** (including **packaging**) or **Six P's** (**people**).

55

FREE Shipping

on orders over $25

If you can't do free, do cheap.

Older businesses can be caught off-guard by the giveaway policies of newer businesses, for example, newspapers that struggle to compete with online providers of free news content. But free has long been widely used in marketing: free admission before 7 p.m.; buy two, get one free; children eat free when accompanied by (hungry, paying) adults.

No giveaway is truly free, so make sure it helps sell your core product. Adobe gives away its PDF Reader software but charges for its Acrobat program that allows one to create and edit PDF documents. Google offers a free stripped-down version of its SketchUp drawing program, from which users build basic skills that create demand for the high-powered subscription version.

If you can't do free, try doing inexpensive, in which case your secondary product might behave as a core product. Printer manufacturers, for example, often sell their printers below or near cost, knowing that buyers will return again and again to buy refill cartridges.

56

One ad, one message.

Conveying too much information in one advertisement, no matter how accurate or positive, can confuse the audience and weaken the message. It's better to tell potential customers one thing that they are likely to find important about a product than everything that may be important. Further, an ad campaign featuring different ads with different information in each may reach a wider audience, as those who overlook one ad might respond positively to another.

57

JUST DO IT.

JUST DO IT.

JUST DO IT.

JUST DO IT.

f Repost this to
avoid seeing the
same people in
your news feed
all the time.

Repetition effect

increasing likelihood of
remembering something
that is repeated often

Illusory truth effect

increasing likelihood of
believing false information
after multiple exposures

Mere exposure effect

inclination to become more
accepting of that to which
one is repeatedly exposed

Repetition doesn't make a statement true, but it can make it believable.

Repetition is an effective way of learning because it hammers information into our memories. Even a false statement, repeated often, can be perceived as true. The **mere exposure effect** is why advertisements are often effective in changing beliefs and attitudes about products and brands, and is a major reason for repetition in advertising.

Producers

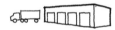

Intermediaries
- promote and advertise products
- match quantities to market needs
- negotiate prices and terms
- store, finance, and transport inventories
- assume risks of theft, damage, and obsolescence

Consumers

Are retailers and wholesalers necessary?

Wouldn't it be better for everyone if all products were sold directly by producers to consumers, bypassing the markups of distributors, wholesalers, and retailers?

No. If chewing gum, for example, were not sold through intermediaries, a manufacturer would have to sell individual packs of gum to each person who wanted one. It is estimated that nearly 400 billion sticks of gum are sold annually. If packaged in tens, manufacturers would have to sell 40 billion packs separately—an impossible task!

59

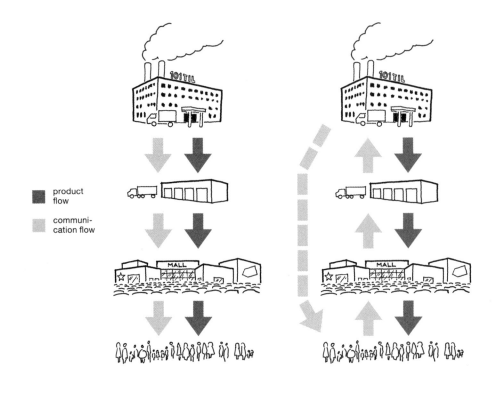

product
flow

communi-
cation flow

Push marketing   Pull marketing

Push for impulse. Pull for brand loyalty.

In **push strategies,** manufacturers promote their product to intermediaries by offering, for example, free in-store promotional displays and price discounts, in an effort to get them to carry and promote the product to consumers. Push strategies are most effective when an item is an impulse purchase, brand loyalty is low, or consumers already understand a product's benefits.

In **pull strategies,** the manufacturer promotes their product directly to consumers, perhaps by providing coupons and free samples, to encourage them to request the item from retailers. This strategy works best when brand loyalty is high and consumers perceive differences between brands.

Secondary
products

Core product

Extend, but don't overextend.

A good brand is recognizable and meaningful to consumers—perhaps signifying emotional security, quality, reliability, safety, aesthetics, lifestyle identity, or environmental sustainability.

   Consumer familiarity can lead to faster acceptance when a company introduces a product in a new category. Ideally, a **brand extension** draws on and supports consumers' existing understanding and image of the brand and its products. If a new product is too different from the brand's existing products—for example, motorcycle manufacturer Harley-Davidson's onetime introduction of a wine cooler—confusion may result, and the brand image may be at least temporarily tarnished.

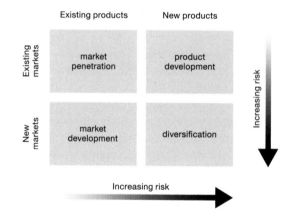

After the Ansoff Matrix by Igor Ansoff

Compete in existing markets and anticipate new ones.

One might envision a business's future as a better version of the current business. This may limit opportunities for expansion into new and related industries. For example, a cable TV company that defines itself as providing television programming might be framing its future too narrowly. By defining its mission more broadly, as the transfer of information to and from homes, it can position itself to provide internet, home security, home automation, and telephone services using the same cable.

62

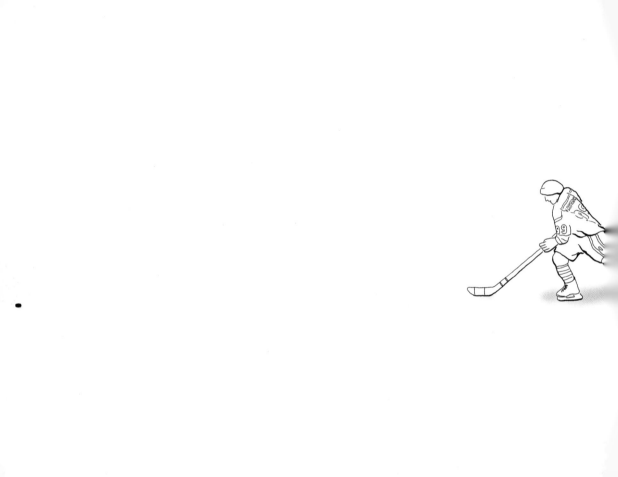

"I skate to where the puck is going to be, not where it has been."

—Attributed to WAYNE GRETZKY, former hockey star

63

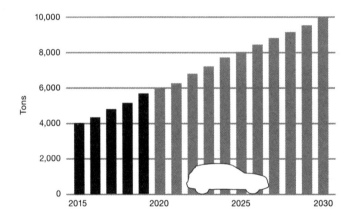

Global use of carbon fiber composites in automobiles
Source: IHS Chemical

Substitutes are competitors.

When evaluating competitors, consider indirect competition as carefully as direct competition. Competition from substitutes can occur at many levels, including product, ingredient, service, and convenience. Plastic, for example, is a common product or ingredient substitute for metal, glass, and ceramics, and thereby competes with them. Grocery stores providing take-out food are convenience substitutes for traditional fast-food restaurants. Even a clothesline is a substitute competitor for a clothes dryer.

64

Functional obsolescence

Technological obsolescence

Obsolete can still be useful.

Functional obsolescence means a device can no longer perform its intended function or cannot perform it efficiently or safely, and should be replaced.

Technological obsolescence means that new technologies have superseded old technologies; however, the older device may still perform reliably, quickly, and safely. Although having the latest and best is appealing, it is often better to push old technology to its limits than to feel obligated to invest in the new.

65

Cannibalize your own sales.

Cannibalization occurs when a company introduces a new or improved product that decreases the sales of its existing products. But it is better to suffer a loss at one's own hands than to have a competitor introduce a product that takes away those same sales.

When introducing an improved product, consider continuing to sell the old product. It usually can be sold at a considerably lower price, because its design, tooling, and other development costs have been covered. This gives customers the option of buying the old product at a low price or the better one at a higher price. It is important, however, that the new product clearly offers something the older one does not, to prevent confusion or resentment among customers.

66

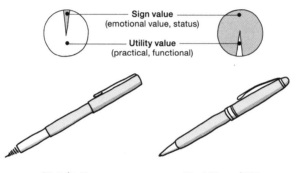

Sign value
(emotional value, status)

Utility value
(practical, functional)

Pilot: $1.49

Mont Blanc: $450

Base your prices on value to the customer, not on your costs.

It's vital to know the costs of bringing a product or service to a customer, as well as the competition's pricing. But customers are unlikely to know a business's costs or markup on what it provides. A business therefore shouldn't base its prices on markups it thinks customers will deem reasonable. It should instead base them on the customers' perceptions of the value provided.

Perception of value can be particularly variable in service industries. For example, a graphic design firm that creates a logo for a multinational corporation provides much greater value than a similar logo for a small indie store. The small business might use it on a store sign, shopping bags, and customer receipts, but the large organization may feature it at every scale from business cards to convention banners to billboards, and in every medium from clothing crests to television commercials.

67

How to run a meeting

Prepare. Create and distribute an agenda three to seven days in advance. Put the highest priority items at the top. Let the participants know your expectations of them so they can prepare.

Consider designating someone to keep notes or minutes and watch the time, if appropriate.

Manage time and behavior. Begin punctually. Encourage participation and debate by all, but if necessary set a limit for how long each person may speak. Cut off debate if it becomes repetitive.

Honor the agenda. Review at the outset of the meeting and ask if any changes are needed. Keep discussion on topic.

68

Draw clear conclusions. Vote on discussion items when appropriate.

Outline the next actions to be taken by the group (things to do, next meeting, etc.). Provide a brief recap and reiterate assigned tasks.

Distribute notes or minutes promptly. Organize them in a format similar to the agenda. Include the major discussion points and the conclusions reached. Solicit comments, questions, corrections, and clarifications.

Form, storm, norm, perform.

Group facilitation helps people with diverse interests forge common goals. Professional facilitators usually know little about the fields in which they consult, but are expert in helping others forge a common direction. They are neutral; they lead discussion and debate but not outcomes. One popular sequence of facilitation is:

Form: Organize the event; discuss the agenda; set expectations and ground rules; establish a schedule; outline the problem and the desired goals.

Storm: Brainstorm and record as many observations, ideas, strategies, and solutions as possible from all participants. Don't critique; record all ideas, even those that appear unlikely to work.

Norm: Discuss implications of the storming alternatives; identify common patterns and areas of overlap; categorize by similarity; identify hierarchies.

69

Perform: Help the group agree on a solution or course of action; determine what needs to be done next.

Facilitation is not linear, however. Smaller F-S-N-P cycles may be found within each phase. As well, groups frequently acquire new insights and/or regress during the Perform stage, and must return to an earlier stage.

Effective speakers know their subject *and* their audience.

What does the audience already know? The answer will tell you where to begin your presentation. By starting with a recap of shared knowledge or concerns, the audience will feel grounded and will be more receptive to new knowledge and alternative points of view.

What is at stake for the audience? A speaker can easily assume that matters of importance to them are of equal concern to listeners. But audiences usually need to be shown what they have at stake. A presentation will be most effective if the audience and speaker have common stakes.

70

What does the audience need? Do they need information or inspiration? Do they need the next increment in their learning, or an expansive presentation that goes far beyond their current knowledge? And among the new material, what is the single, crucial takeaway?

The point of a visual presentation is to get the audience to *listen.*

It can be tempting to pack slides or presentation boards with extra information to look smart or give the audience extra value. But the most effective visual presentations are clear, concise, and even terse. Limit text on visual props to a few lines or bullet points; five or six is usually the maximum. Never read slides to the audience; use other words to reinforce and expand on the point being made. When using presentation software, reveal the lines as you speak them. Otherwise, the audience will stop listening to you while they read your slide. If you have additional details to convey, put them in a takeaway handout or send them afterward in a thank-you e-mail.

71

Litigation
- usually either/or outcome
- most formal
- most expensive
- most stressful
- public result

Arbitration
- may have either/or outcome
- formal
- some flexibility
- very stressful
- public or private result

Mediation
- may seek middle ground
- usually more informal
- most flexible
- stressful, but less than others
- private result

Dispute resolution

The party that cares less has the stronger bargaining position.

There is no stronger position at a negotiating table than indifference—to be able to walk away without negative consequence. This is not to say that a walk-away strategy is the best in every circumstance or over the long run; one can win many individual negotiating battles but lose a larger negotiating effort by alienating those with whom business could otherwise have been done in the future. One might even bring harm to *both* parties.

Win-win negotiating aims to impart mutual satisfaction through meta-strategies: Is there a higher level of engaging the impasse at which everyone can get an acceptable version of what they want? Are each party's needs truly exclusive of the other's? Does each party know what is most important to it? Is each holding on to what is most to its benefit, and willing to let go of what is not?

With regards to Professor Patrick Liles

There's a trolley every 15 minutes.

The opportunity in front of you may seem once-in-a-lifetime. But opportunities are numerous. It is usually better to wait for or seek another than to rush into one without performing due diligence—whether buying a car, house, or company. A successful entry into a bad venture may be far worse than missing out entirely on a good venture.

"You can always recover from the player you didn't sign. You may never recover from the player you signed at the wrong price."

—BILLY BEANE, executive vice president of baseball operations for the Oakland A's, as quoted in *Moneyball* by Michael Lewis

74

Survival for small brick-and-mortar retail

Glom on. Locate near complementary businesses, taking note of common audience needs at specific times of day, e.g., a dry cleaner near a coffee shop (mornings), or a takeout dinner restaurant near a daycare facility (evenings).

Get signage right. Don't cram limited sign space with complex images or hard-to-read fonts that obfuscate your core business. For visibility in urban locations, try mounting an exterior sign perpendicular to the facade, if allowed.

Scale window displays to the context. A delicate jewelry display may be effective on a busy pedestrian way, but it will disappear on the front of a strip mall.

Provide transitional space. Design the entry so that arriving customers can exhibit with their body language if they wish to be immediately engaged by staff.

Make the environment immersive. Provide experiences that online retail cannot. Make all merchandise touchable, and offer food, music, community engagement, readings, lectures, and/or product demos in addition to your core products.

Make desired items harder to find, and impulse items easier. Don't bury a high-selling product, but make sure customers engage other products while seeking it.

Remove one or two items from a new display. A perfect display looks like it is not to be disturbed. A not-quite-complete display suggests buying has begun.

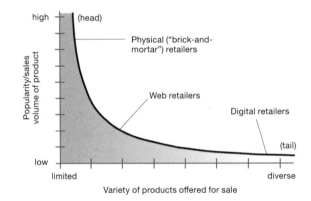

75

Long tail online retail model
With regards to Chris Anderson

Online commerce tends to have a long tail.

Traditional brick-and-mortar stores have limited, expensive floor space compared to online retailers, and stock a relatively narrow range of items, each of which they sell to a small, local customer base in proportionately large quantities.

Online retailers of hard goods do not depend on in-person shoppers and can locate in low-traffic, inexpensive areas. This makes it affordable for them to stock slow-moving as well as popular items, which they sell nationally or globally.

Online digital retailers, which sell digital products over the Web, require almost no warehouse space; the product is stored on a computer hard drive or in the cloud. They have very low inventory costs. This allows them to stock obscure, extremely slow-moving items, which they sell nationally or globally. In transmitting their products digitally, they incur no shipping costs.

76

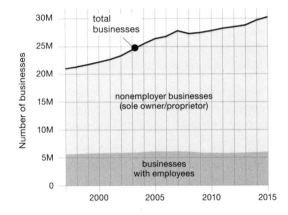

U.S. employer and nonemployer businesses
Sources: U.S. Census Bureau and Small Business Association

Without small businesses, there would be no large businesses.

Large, multinational businesses have capabilities that small, local businesses do not. But small businesses also perform important economic functions. Studies show that money spent in a locally owned business has 2 to 4 times the impact on the local economy as the same amount spent at a corporate chain.

The vast majority of businesses in the United States are small and local. In fact, *every* business, at some point in its lineage, was a small, local business.

77

Two retail giants grow from a yard sale

In 1873 in Wheaton, Illinois, Reverend Charles Barnes decided to sell some books from his home library. The success of the sale led him to open a retail bookstore in his home.

Three years later, Barnes moved his burgeoning enterprise to Chicago. His son William eventually assumed ownership, which he later passed to Charles Follett, a stock clerk who had risen into management. William Barnes moved to New York City, and with Gilbert Noble established the Barnes & Noble bookstore chain in 1917. Meanwhile, in Chicago, Charles Follett continued to expand his enterprise by opening bookstores on numerous college campuses.

The two businesses grew throughout the twentieth century. While the original Wheaton store is long gone, and the zoning of the neighborhood now forbids retail businesses, an ad hoc startup in a home ultimately helped create two major corporations. Today, Barnes & Noble and Follett Corporation operate nearly 3,000 general and college bookstores, and generate nearly $7B in total annual revenue.

78

"All people are entrepreneurs, but many don't have the opportunity to find that out."

—MUHAMMAD YUNUS, founder of the Grameen Bank and Nobel Peace Prize winner

79

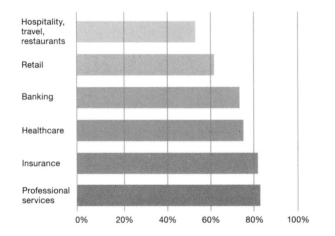

Customer retention rates in selected industries worldwide, 2018
Source: Statista

Don't let one customer dictate your business.

Acquiring new customers can be difficult and expensive, so one might be inclined to try to hang on to all of his existing customers. But some might not be worth it. Many customers will value a business's products or services, know how to use them, respect the company's time and attention, and buy in reasonable quantities, but others will make unreasonable demands, have a constant stream of returns, and be slow in paying, all while buying in quantities too small for the business to be profitable.

Big customers also can become detrimental. Their large, consistent purchases can grant predictability, profitability, and economies of scale, but losing them can be devastating. A customer whose regular purchases constitute a disproportion of a business's sales, and who is aware of his or her consequent power, may demand that the business lower its prices to an unreasonable level. An especially aggressive customer may even threaten to stop all purchases if not allowed to buy the entire business at a bargain price.

Complaining customers want to keep doing business with you.

Most customers who complain about a business don't want to end their relationship with it; they just want something to change. Customers whose complaints are resolved quickly and satisfactorily often become very loyal, become personally attached to the business and its employees, provide positive word of mouth, and make larger purchases. They may even pay more for the product or service.

There are costs to resolving complaints, but recruiting new customers usually costs more than retaining existing customers. And for every customer who complains, many unsatisfied customers quietly leave and never come back. A complaining customer ultimately saves a business money.

"Your most unhappy customers are your greatest source of learning."

—BILL GATES, co-founder of Microsoft Corporation, *Business @ the Speed of Thought*

82

Offer and acceptance
firm, unambiguous; "meeting
of the minds" on all terms

Consideration
something of value
exchanged

Legal intent
lawfully entered and
in proper legal form

Competence
parties understand
their obligations

Components of a contract

Write it once.

A well-written contract defines or explains each term or condition only once. Subsequent mentions of that term or condition refer to, or are presumed to refer to, the original explanation. Repeating contract language in an effort to impart greater emphasis is dangerous, as differences in context can lead to confusion in meaning and an unfavorable interpretation in a court of law. Further, because negotiations invariably require the editing of a contract draft, a redundantly worded document will require changes in multiple locations—leading to the possibility that one location will be missed and an inconsistent final contract will result.

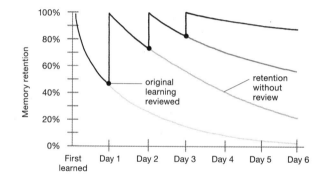

Ebbinghaus forgetting curve

Say it twice.

No matter how clear we are in our verbal communications, misunderstandings occur. To minimize them, end conversations and meetings with a summary of conclusions, including the participants' responsibilities and the next steps to be taken. Saying things a bit differently the second time often helps reinforce a message and uncover misunderstandings.

When assigning a new task, ask the assignee to demonstrate in writing, if simply a brief e-mail, their understanding of it. This will give both parties an opportunity to correct any misunderstandings before they impair performance.

do it better

less achievable

more achievable

get more done

Do fewer things, but do them better.

Business owners, managers, employees, and students can become overwhelmed, distracted, and frustrated by trying to do too many things well. When having difficulty maintaining quality standards, achieving desired outcomes, meeting schedule and cost targets, or getting others to prioritize and perform well, try reducing the number of things being attempted, and focus on doing those fewer things better.

There are important tasks that must be done promptly, unimportant tasks that must be done promptly, important tasks with no particular rush, and unimportant tasks with no particular rush; and sometimes there are things that seem crucial but may not need doing at all.

85

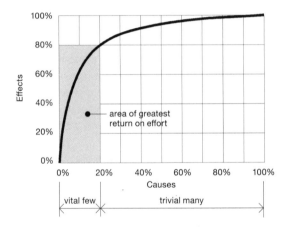

The Pareto Principle

Sacrifice the trivial many for the vital few.

The **Pareto Principle,** a concept created by Joseph Juran, says that 20% of causes are usually responsible for 80% of results. This suggests that businesses are best served by giving the most attention to the 20% of customers accounting for 80% of its sales, to the 20% of efforts that will achieve 80% of the outcomes, or to solving the 20% of factors causing 80% of its problems. Some will even argue that 80% of the work in an organization is done by 20% of its people.

86

Variations on the triangle

Quality, price, service: pick two.

The quality of a product, its price, and the level of service its seller provides are interdependent. No seller can offer the best of all three—highest quality, lowest price, and best service—and remain in business. A discount store that offers high-quality merchandise at low prices will necessarily provide minimal personal service. A store selling the same merchandise with a high level of attention from staff will charge a higher price.

In project management, three similar factors are in play: quality, price, and time; one can prioritize only two of them. And if one of the factors is changed after the project is begun—a suddenly tighter schedule, a demand for better (or more) work, or a budget cut—you must change two of them: A request for higher quality means one will have to pay more or expand the schedule. An accelerated schedule will require paying more or accepting lower quality. A reduced budget will mean a slower schedule or reduced quality.

Risk appetite
willingness or desire
to take a risk

Risk tolerance
ability to manage the
downside of a risk

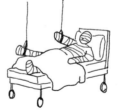

Risk seeks its own level.

Risk homeostasis theory says that people have an innate sense of the level of risk they consider acceptable in a given activity. When the activity is made safer, they behave more recklessly, at least partly nullifying the safety gains.

A study at the University of Bath found that drivers drove measurably closer to bicyclists who were wearing helmets than those without helmets. Another study found that Munich taxicab drivers of vehicles with antilock brakes took corners faster and left shorter reaction zones than drivers of cabs with conventional brakes. The two groups ultimately had the same crash rate.

88

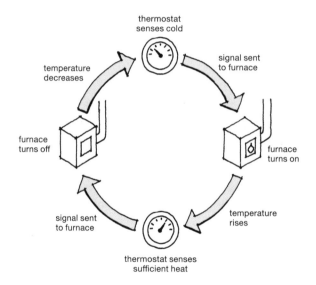

thermostat
senses cold

signal sent
to furnace

temperature
decreases

furnace
turns on

furnace
turns off

temperature
rises

signal sent
to furnace

thermostat senses
sufficient heat

A negative feedback loop

Positive and negative feedback loops

In a **negative feedback loop,** a system responds in the opposite direction of a stimulus, thereby providing overall stability or equilibrium. The Law of Supply and Demand usually functions as a negative feedback loop: when the supply of a product, material, or service increases, its price tends to fall, which may lead to rising demand, which will drive the price back up.

In a **positive feedback loop,** a system responds in the same direction as the stimulus, decreasing equilibrium further and further. For example, a consumer who feels prosperous after making new purchases may end up making even more purchases and take on excessive debt. Eventually, the consumer may face financial ruin and have to make a major correction by selling off assets or declaring bankruptcy. Because positive feedback loops often lead to a dramatic restoration of equilibrium, it is sometimes suggested that they exist within a larger, if not directly visible, negative feedback loop.

The Law of Supply and Demand doesn't always apply.

The familiar **Law of Supply and Demand** says that if the supply of a given product or service exceeds demand, its price will decrease; if demand exceeds supply, its price will increase. Increases and decreases in price affect demand in the same way. When supply and demand are exactly equal, the market is at equilibrium and acts most efficiently: suppliers sell all the goods they produce and consumers get all the goods they demand.

Not all products adhere to the Law, however. When the prices of some luxury or prestige items have been lowered, demand for them has fallen due to consumers perceiving reduced cachet. In other instances, rising demand for a product has led to improvements in technology, production, and distribution, driving prices down. Electronic and digital technologies have often followed this pattern.

90

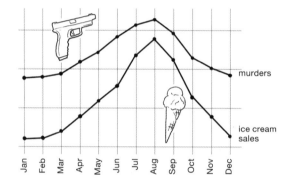

murders

ice cream
sales

Jan Feb Mar Apr May Jun Jul Aug Sep Oct Nov Dec

Correlation isn't necessarily causation.

Beginning in 1924, the Hawthorne Studies were conducted at Western Electric Company in Cicero, Illinois. Various environmental changes were introduced to determine their effects on worker efficiency. Initial improvements were thought to be due to changes in lighting, work hours, and break times. However, it became apparent that almost every change in the environment, even the reintroduction of a previous condition, increased productivity. Later theorists posited that the workers worked better simply because they knew they were being observed.

The Hawthorne Studies, still debated today, gave their name to the **Hawthorne effect,** also called the **observer effect,** by which individuals under study modify their behavior because of their awareness of the study.

Unregistered trademark	TM	May or may not be protectable
Design patent	👓	14 years
Utility patent	⚙️	20 years
Copyright	©	Life of creator + 50 to 70 years
Registered trademark	®	No expiration if remaining in use

Typical duration of protection

Intellectual property protection

Trademark: a distinctive word, phrase, image, sound, fragrance, or combination used by an individual or business to distinguish its goods. Registration with the U.S. Patent and Trademark Office results in formal legal ownership and is indicated by ®. The symbol ™ indicates an unregistered trademark for products, while ^SM indicates an unregistered mark for services.

Patent: a protection granted by the USPTO allowing an inventor to exclude others from making, using, offering for sale, or importing the same invention. A **utility patent** grants legal ownership of a functional improvement to a product, and prevents others from copying or using it without permission. A **design patent** protects aesthetic or ornamental elements.

Copyright: Registration with the U.S. Copyright Office generally protects literary, musical, dramatic, pictorial, artistic, and architectural works; motion pictures; musical compositions; sound recordings; software; and radio and television broadcasts. Only the tangible expression of an idea, not an idea itself, is copyrightable.

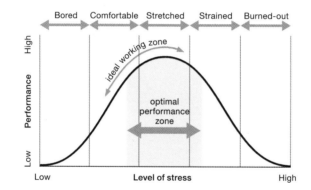

Some stress is good.

Stress has many causes: tight deadlines, financial constraints, demanding customers, aggressive competition, and the expectations of work colleagues. The **Yerkes-Dodson Law** says that performance increases with stress, but only up to a point. When stress is too high, performance decreases.

93

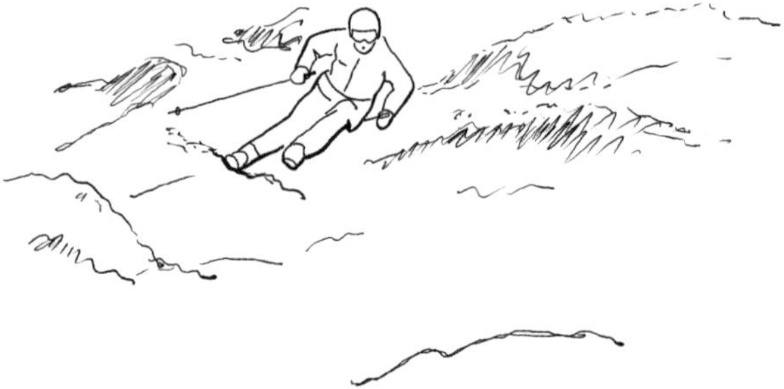

Keep your knees bent.

Change is constant. New competitors appear, existing suppliers disappear. Costs increase, product shortages arise, customers go away without explanation, and valued clients move on to other vendors. Natural disasters, worker strikes, and pandemics occur with little warning. Tariffs and trade policies increase prices overnight.

A crisis is a time of sudden change, and change brings opportunities—although they might lie in places other than where you preferred or were inclined to look. A hurricane wreaks destruction, but it will create a demand for plywood before it strikes and additional building materials afterward. A pandemic may force people to stay at home, but there will be greater demand for medical gear and food delivery. A trade war may produce drastic cost increases or material scarcities, but new sources will crop up that may form the basis for lifelong working partnerships.

"Two basic rules of life are:
 1) Change is inevitable.
 2) Everybody resists change."

—W. EDWARDS DEMING, management consultant (1900–1993)

95

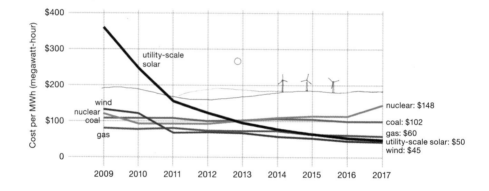

North American levelized energy costs
Source: Lazard's Levelized Cost of Energy Analysis, 2017

Going green can make more "green."

Sustainable practices have often been embraced more for ecological concern than economic benefit. Alternative energy systems, for example, usually have high capital costs compared to conventional systems, and may seem an unnecessary expense. But they almost always have lower operating costs and are more economical in the long run. For example, it will cost more to install a geothermal heating system in a building than an oil- or gas-fueled system. But once the infrastructure is paid for, geothermal energy is nearly free.

An analysis of the lifetime costs of all energy sources suggests that nearly all alternative fuels are less expensive than fossil fuels.

96

Banks make
high-risk loans

Many loans
not repaid

Government
bails out banks

Banks do not
suffer losses

Moral hazard

A **moral hazard** exists when organizations and individuals are not required to bear the negative consequences of their failures. Moral hazards can result from a positive feedback loop: for example, a lender that is insured by the government against loan default may make very risky, high-interest loans to uncreditworthy customers because it will do no worse than break even, and may realize a very high rate of return.

97

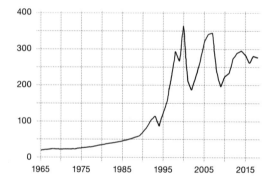

Ratio of for-profit CEO compensation to average employee
Source: Economic Policy Institute

Doing good can lead to doing well.

In 2015, Dan Price, CEO of a Seattle credit card payments company, got an earful from an employee who was struggling to make ends meet. Price reacted defensively, but later thought about his own salary in contrast to those of his workers. He read that the annual salary at which workers worried least about their future was $70,000. Price cut his own pay from $1.1 million to $70,000, and announced a company-wide minimum salary of $70,000—effectively doubling the pay of over one-third of his 120 workers.

Some higher-paid staff disagreed with the policy, and left. But after a period of adjustment, productivity increased. Workers were able to let go of second jobs and focus on doing one job well. Many could afford to live closer to work, and spent less time commuting. Home ownership among employees jumped to 10% from 1%. Good press on Price's actions led to an increase in processing volume from $3.8B to $10.2B in five years, and the doubling of his workforce.

Clan

family-like, mentoring, nurturing, "does things together"

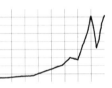

Market-oriented

results/achievement oriented, competitive, "gets the job done"

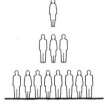

Hierarchy

structured, controlled, efficient, stable, "does things right"

Adhocracy

dynamic, unstructured, risk-taking, innovative, "does things first"

Four types of organizational culture
Source: Robert E. Quinn and Kim S. Cameron, University of Michigan at Ann Arbor

Learn an organization's culture before working with or for it.

Organizational culture is the set of behaviors, norms, attitudes, priorities, and beliefs accepted by and within an organization. Cultures vary widely: In some, executives are aloof, while in others they are more accessible. In some, processes and behaviors are ad hoc and quirky, while in others regimentation and predictability are norms. A poor cultural match can not only create discomfort for workers, but can compromise endeavors at a corporate scale—undermining mergers, partnerships, and working relationships that are a good match by non-cultural measures.

Widget Corporation
Business Plan

Introduction 1

Executive Summary 3

Company Description 6

Products and Services 12

Market Analysis 17

Strategy and Implementation 22

Organization and Management Team 25

Financial Plan and Projections

Passion drives a business; business runs a business.

Many small businesses fail because their owners mistake their passion for a field for a desire to run a business in that field. Successful business owners are passionate but recognize that enthusiasm is not an adequate business plan. They know that the business of business—marketing, financing, hiring, training, firing, planning, negotiating, purchasing, balancing the books, maintaining the physical plant, resolving employee tiffs, and more—must receive primary attention if their passion is to thrive.

100

"We survive by breathing but we can't say we live to breathe. Likewise, making money is very important for a business to survive, but money alone cannot be the reason for business to exist."

—ANU AGA, former chair, Thermax Ltd.

Index

accounting
    cash versus accrual, 17
    debits and credits, 17, 18
    defined, 2
    depreciation, 19
    financial ratios, 21
    matching principle, 19
    reports, 20, 21
adaptability/flexibility, as a
    business skill, Author's
    Note, 13, 32, 36, 94, 95
advertising, 50, 57, 58
Aga, Anu (former chair,
    Thermax Ltd.), 101
alternative energy, 96
Anderson, Chris (author/
    entrepreneur), 76
Ansoff, Igor, 62
Ansoff Matrix, 62
assets, 6, 11, 21

bankruptcy, 6, 29, 30
Barnes, Charles, 78
Barnes & Noble bookstore
    chain, 78
Barnes, William, 78
Beane, Billy (baseball
    executive), 74

board of directors, 6, 7
bonds, 5, 6
borrowing, 5, 24
branding/brand equity/brand
    identity, 11, 50, 51, 61
business
    defined, 1
    forms/ownership, 3, 4, 5, 6
    government regulation
        of, 3, 9
    as a human endeavor, 9
    organization and structure,
        2, 12, 13, 34, 35, 36, 99
        see also management
    owner liability in, 4
    philosophy, 9
    size, 4, 12, 77, 78 see also
        small business
    social/moral
        responsibilities of, 7,
        9, 97, 98

Cameron, Kim S.
    (management
    professor), 99
capital, 5, 11, 29
cash flow, 20, 21, 29
causation, vs. correlation, 91
CEO compensation, 98

Coca-Cola, 66
communication, 45, 84
competition, 64, 66, 67
contracts, 83
Costco, 21
costs
    fixed, 28
    fixed and variable, 23
    material and labor, 22
Cox, Harvey (theologian), 44
customers
    business relationship with,
        52, 80, 81, 82
    reasons for making a
        purchase, 53, 55

Damodaran, Aswath (business
    professor), 3
debentures, 6
debt, 31
deflation, 28
Deming, W. Edwards
    (management consultant),
    95
dispute resolution, 72
Dow Jones Industrial Average,
    27

Ebbinghaus forgetting
    curve, 84
economics, defined, 2
employees
    compensation, 14
    hiring, 14
    motivation, 47, 48, 49
    promotion/advancement
        within organization,
        14, 45
    satisfaction, 14
entrepreneurship, 77, 78, 79
environmental responsibility,
    7, 96
equity, 5, 11, 20, 21
expertise, 35, 39, 45

Facebook, 8
feedback loop, 89, 90, 97
finance, 2, 29
Follett, Charles, 78
Follett Corporation, 78
Four P's, 55

Gates, Bill (co-founder of
    Microsoft Corporation), 82
General Motors, 54
Gerber, Michael (business
    consultant and author), 16
Grameen Bank, 79
Gretzky, Wayne (hockey
    star), 63
group facilitation, 69

harassment in workplace, 15
Harley-Davidson, 61
Hawthorne Studies, 91
Honda, 54

illusory truth effect, 58
inflation, 28
intellectual property, 92
interest rate, 24, 25
intermediaries, 59

Japanese Consumer Price
    Index, 28
Juran, Joseph (management
    consultant), 86

Law of Supply and
    Demand, 90
leadership, 8
Lewin, Kurt (psychologist), 33
Liles, Patrick, 73

management
    decision-making, 37, 38,
        40, 41, 42, 43
    delegation, 45, 46, 47, 48,
        49, 84
    micromanagement, 47
    people problems, 15
    setting and managing
        priorities, 85, 86, 87
    in small businesses, 75,
        100
    team building, 45

    top-down and
        bottom-up, 35
    manager behavior, 15, 16
marketing, 2, 50, 54, 56, 60,
    61, 62, 63
meeting, how to run, 68
mere exposure effect, 58
mission statement, 10
monopoly, regulated, 3
Mont Blanc pen, 67
moral hazard, 97

negotiation, 72, 73, 74
Noble, Gilbert, 78

obsolescence, 65
opportunity, 42, 73, 74
organizational behavior and
    culture, 2, 99

Pareto Principle, 86
performance analysis, 21
Pilot pen, 67
Price, Dan
    (businessperson), 98
prices/pricing of products
    and services, 11, 56,
    67, 90
products
    core and secondary,
        56, 61
    development and
        diversification, 62
    features/benefits, 53

promotion and publicity, 50
public speaking, 70, 71

quality-price-service
	triangle, 87
Quinn, Robert E.
	(management
	consultant), 99

repetition effect, 58
retailers, 59, 60, 75, 76, 78
risk homeostasis, 88
Rule of 72, 25

sales, 52, 53, 56, 60, 66
Sandberg, Sheryl (COO,
	Facebook), 8

satisficers, vs. maximizers, 43
small business, 4, 12, 67, 77,
	78, 79, 100
span of control, 34
Steward, David L.
	(businessperson), 49
stocks/stockholders/stock
	market, 4, 5, 6, 27
stress, performance
	under, 93
Subaru, 54

theory, purpose of,
	32, 33
Toyota, 54

U.S. Federal Reserve, 26

U.S. government, fiscal and
	monetary policy, 26

value of goods and services,
	1, 11, 67
vision statement, 10

Walmart, 20, 21
website design, 51
wholesalers, 59

Yerkes-Dodson Law, 93
Yunus, Muhammad (founder,
	Grameen Bank), 79

Michael W. Preis has been a management consultant, business owner, executive, and clinical professor of business administration at the University of Illinois at Urbana-Champaign. He holds a BS in mechanical engineering from The Ohio State University, an MBA from Harvard Business School, and a PhD in marketing from George Washington University.

Matthew Frederick is a business owner, bestselling author, instructor of design and writing, and the creator of the 101 Things I Learned® series. He lives in New York's Hudson Valley.